ONE WAS LEFT ALIVE

ONE WAS LEFT ALIVE

Jenny Tripp

Illustrated by John Burgoyne

RAINTREE PUBLISHERS
Milwaukee • Toronto • Melbourne • London

Copyright © 1980, Raintree Publishers Inc.

All rights reserved. No part of this book may be reproduced
or utilized in any form or by any means, electronic or mechanical,
including photocopying, recording, or by any information storage
and retrieval system, without permission in writing from the
Publisher. Inquiries should be addressed to Raintree Publishers Inc.,
205 West Highland Avenue, Milwaukee, Wisconsin 53203.

Library of Congress Number: 79-21150

2 3 4 5 6 7 8 9 0 84 83 82 81

Printed and bound in the United States of America.

Library of Congress Cataloging in Publication Data

Tripp, Jenny.
  One was left alive.

  SUMMARY: Describes the ordeal faced by the sole
survivor of a 1971 airplane crash in the Peruvian
jungle.
    1. Survival (after airplane accidents, shipwrecks,
etc.) — Juvenile literature. 2. Aeronautics — Accidents —
1971 — Juvenile literature. 3. Koepcke, Juliane.
[1. Survival. 2. Aeronautics — Accidents.
3. Koepcke, Juliane] I. Burgoyne, John. II. Title.
TL553.9.T74   985   79-21150
ISBN 0-8172-1555-7 lib. bdg.

CONTENTS

CHAPTER 1

Everything Grew Dark

The day before Christmas, 1971, dawned hot and sunny in Lima, Peru. Juliane Koepcke and her mother were leaving that day on Flight 508 for Pucallpa. This is a tiny town in the jungle. It lies 475 miles north of Lima, across the high Andes Mountains.

Juliane was excited. Christmas was almost here and she had just graduated from high school in Peru. She and her mother were going to join her father to spend a family Christmas together in their jungle hut.

Both her parents had come to Peru from Germany twenty-five years before. Her father wanted to study animals and plants. Her mother would study the many colorful birds of the jungle. Both were teachers at the University of Lima. As she grew up, Juliane had spent a lot of time in the jungle with her parents.

That day before Christmas, Juliane had many

happy things to think about. She thought about the holiday, gifts, her future now that she'd finished school, and the bright new dress she was wearing. She and her mother joked and chatted happily as they walked through the airport. The airport bustled with smiling people. Many of them carried packages wrapped in bright paper. And it was a perfect day for flying. The winter sky held no clouds.

On the plane, Juliane took a window seat. Her mother sat in the middle seat. A man they didn't know had the seat on the aisle. They would arrive in Pucallpa about forty minutes after takeoff.

After the plane was in the air, the stewardesses

passed out coffee and sweet rolls. Everyone relaxed.

Then, without warning, everything grew dark. A sudden storm had come up. Angry black clouds blotted out the sun. Rain pounded against the plane's windows. No one could see land, only rain.

The plane shuddered and shook, bouncing up and down. Nervous passengers began to call for the stewardesses. They moved quickly to comfort the passengers. Bright flashes of lightning lit the terror-stricken faces, and the plane shook harder.

Then the passengers heard the pilot's voice. The storm would pass as quickly as it had come, the pilot promised. Everything would be all right.

Juliane's mother reached over the armrest and patted her daughter's hand. But under her smile Juliane could sense her mother's alarm. She herself began to feel afraid. She glanced at the passengers across from her, a group of young girls, now pale and silent. In front of them an old couple sat. They held each other's hands around the packages they had brought on board. Juliane tightened her seatbelt as much as she could.

Hand luggage, held in racks overhead, now began to fall onto the floor. The plane jarred and jerked like a landed fish. A woman screamed as her parcels fell on her.

All at once, a terrible bolt of lightning lighted

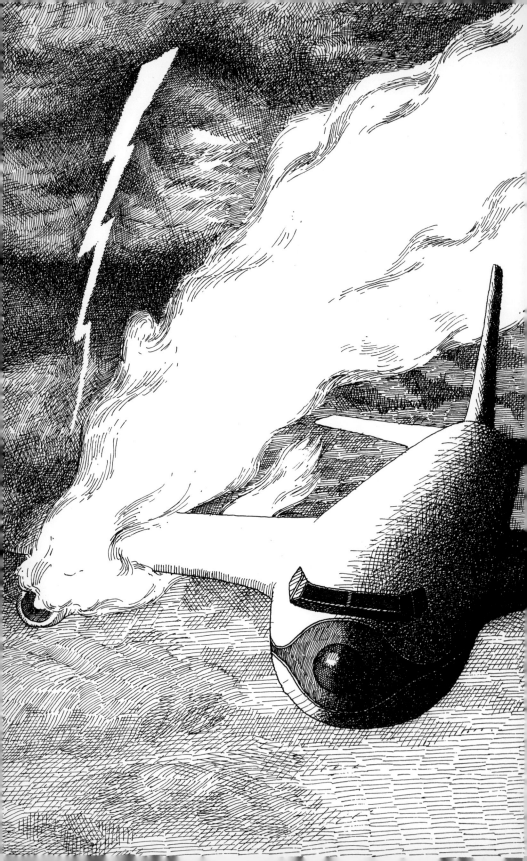

the darkness around the plane. Inside, the screams grew louder. Juliane glanced out of the window. She saw something that made her heart leap. Bright orange and yellow flames flared from the right wing! Her mother turned to her and said calmly, "This is the end of everything."

The plane gave a great lurch. There was a roaring in Juliane's ears, and she closed her eyes. She was certain she was going to die. Seconds later, she opened her eyes.

Astonishingly, Juliane found herself falling. She was still strapped into her seat and turning over and over. The green jungle below rushed toward her. Her numbed mind noted that the jungle looked a little like cauliflower from that height. Then, Juliane blacked out.

CHAPTER 2

Alive in the Jungle

The ceaseless pat-pat-pat of rain on her face woke Juliane up. Slowly, she tried to think of where she was. She tried to remember what had happened. Faintly at first, then more clearly, she heard the sounds of the jungle around her. The rain fell softly now, striking the carpet of leaves and brush on the jungle floor. Birds called. Frogs croaked in low, regular rhythm. The hum and whir of thousands of insects buzzed in Juliane's ears.

Then Juliane saw a patch of blue sky. She realized with a start that it was still daylight. She couldn't guess how long she had lain there. It finally came to her that she had fallen from the plane as it exploded in midair. Somehow she was still alive. Her head pounded. She had trouble seeing. Juliane tried to move. She checked her arms and legs and made sure she was still in one

piece. She was still strapped into her seat, and the seat was still upside down. The seat was still connected to the two others. They were empty.

Juliane realized that she had lived through a miracle. But a stab of terror pierced her when she remembered that she was alone. There was no sign of her mother, nor of any other survivors.

Her body felt strange, sort of tingly. But shortly the numbness gave way to feelings of pain. There was a bump on her head that was growing larger. One eye was swelling shut rapidly from a blow near her eyebrow. Juliane figured that she wouldn't be able to see out of that eye when the bruise grew larger. She felt something warm dripping down her foot. She realized it was blood, coming from a gash. She couldn't tell how badly she was cut. Juliane noticed that her glasses were missing. So was one of her shoes. She wiggled her fingers. She noticed that one of the several rings she had been wearing was gone too. She felt lucky she still had her hands.

Shock stole over her, making her sleepy. Juliane knew that she should try to free herself from the seatbelt and push the seats off her. Somewhere, there might be other survivors. Somewhere, her mother might be trapped as she was, needing help. But when she tried to get out, she found that she was too weak to make it. She felt as helpless as a baby. Her body refused to obey her commands. And she found herself growing more sleepy, lulled by the wild birds' songs and the still falling rain.

Even as she drifted off into a deep sleep, she wondered what would become of her. Would she live to wake up?

Juliane slept through the long night. She awoke at dawn. Today, she knew, she must rise. To let exhaustion settle over her again, to go back to sleep, would mean death. After working on the seatbelt, Juliane crawled slowly out from under the seats. She squinted in the light. Her eyes swam with dizziness as she rose unsteadily to her feet. She looked around her.

On the ground nearby, she saw a white cardboard box, wrapped and tied with string. She walked over to it, and bent stiffly to pick it up. Her hands seemed to move slowly. It took her several minutes to tear open the package. Inside

the box she found a cake and some bright, hard candy. Her eyes misted over with tears. Here was someone's Christmas present to a loved one they would never see again. The colorful Christmas candies seemed strangely out of place in the soggy jungle. But it was food, and she knew she had to eat if she were to survive. Juliane pulled off a piece of the cake and put it in her mouth. She gagged and spat it out. It was waterlogged and sickening. Even if she were starving, she knew she couldn't stomach it. But the candies were all right. They were wet but still hard. She put them in the pocket of her dress.

Juliane remembered what her father had taught her in their years in the jungle. The jungle is hard on those who don't fit there. It is full of

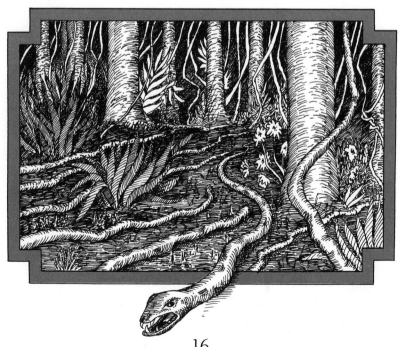

16

danger. Ocelots in black-ringed yellow coats prowl for snakes, birds, and small animals. Spotted jaguars in their tawny hides blend into the sun-speckled forest floor or into the trees in which they crouched. These big cats hunt larger animals—deer, rabbit-sized creatures called agouti, and ferocious, sharp-tusked peccaries, wild pigs that fight fiercly when cornered. Juliane herself would be easy prey for the big cats, she knew.

Even more dangerous to her than the big animals, were the small ones with which the jungle teemed. There were many poisonous snakes and stinging insects. The trees also held great anacondas. These are brightly colored snakes that sometimes grow to twenty-five feet in length. They capture their prey by stunning it with a sudden strike of their fangs. Then they wrap their strong bodies around the animal and squeeze the life out of it. Then they swallow it whole. Smaller snakes could also be dangerous. The fer-de-lance, a kind of pit viper, is usually five or six feet long. But its powerful poison makes it a deadly danger. The fer-de-lance can feel the approach of warm-blooded prey without seeing it. The snake's gray-brown markings allow it to hide among the twisted vines on the jungle floor.

Now Juliane searched around her. Soon she spotted what she was looking for—a long stick straight enough to lean on and sharp at one end.

Juliane would use the stick to poke the ground before her as she walked. That way she could drive out snakes that might be hiding.

The terrors of the jungle were great. But even worse was the terror of being alone, of simply waiting to die. Juliane knew she must go out into the dangerous, steamy jungle world if she were to stand a chance of living. And she had to find her mother. Juliane began to walk.

CHAPTER 3

I've Got to Get Back

Juliane's walk through the hot, wet jungle was slow. She stumbled in the underbrush, her sore foot throbbing with pain. Her head ached. And every few minutes, tired and weak, she had to sit down and rest.

In which direction should she go? She searched her mind for anything her parents might have taught her about the art of survival. Suddenly she remembered something her father had said. "If you ever find yourself lost in the wilderness, the best thing you can do is to find a stream and follow it to a larger stream." Rivers, cutting through the jungle, were the main "roads" for people who lived in villages. Indians built their huts close to a river. They fished in it and traveled on it in their canoes. Juliane would need water to drink, too. She walked, pausing every now and then to rest and listen carefully for a sound of running water.

And then she heard it, a soft splashing that seemed to be coming from just a few yards away. Carefully picking her way along, Juliane followed the sound, which grew louder and louder. Then she found it, a tiny brook washing swiftly over the stones in its bed.

Juliane thought for a moment. Then she decided to follow the stream. Streams in the jungle often wander and circle wildly. To follow this one might mean that she'd walk miles along its banks without really getting ahead more than a few hundred yards. And there was a whole new set of enemies now. Huge mosquitoes attacked her as she moved along the stream's bank. She slapped at them wildly. But soon her body began to show their bites.

The stream's bank was overgrown with vines and other plants. This made the going rough. Sometimes Juliane could not get through. She had to step into the stream to get past a fallen tree or a limb barring the way. Her heart leaped when she remembered that her bloody foot might be bait for tiny, razor-toothed piranhas. Piranhas are small fish, but their powerful jaws can strip a human or a cow of flesh in minutes. And the logs resting in the water often seemed like caimans, huge lumbering alligators.

As she continued to pick her way carefully along, Juliane's ears picked up a new sound. She

shook her head, thinking her tiredness might be playing tricks on her ears. But the sound, a buzzing hum, didn't go away. It grew louder, nearer. She would investigate it.

Juliane let her ears lead her toward the sound. She found herself in a small clearing. Then she spotted something that made her cry out in horror.

Before her lay three seats, torn as hers had been from the airplane. They were upright on the ground. In them sat three girls, all strapped into their seats. All three were dead and covered with flies. They made the buzzing that had drawn Juliane there. Sickened, she turned and stumbled back toward the stream.

The afternoon sunlight coming through the trees gradually dimmed to gold. As the light faded, the mosquitoes grew even thicker. Juliane kept trying to bat them off her face and neck. Sometimes, when she gasped for breath, one would fly into her mouth or nose. This made her cough and spit in disgust. Her nerves seemed to be dulled.

Juliane's mind wandered. She thought back to her childhood and to her graduation day. All that seemed like something from another life. Now, there was only the jungle, the heat, the endless attacks by insects, and the need to be always watchful. She tried not to think of her mother, but thoughts of her would creep into Juliane's mind bringing tears to her bloodshot eyes. What was her father doing? she wondered. Surely news of the crash had reached him by now. She hated to think of him worrying, not knowing. Maybe, she thought, he was better off not knowing.

Now and then Juliane would talk or call out. She hoped that someone might hear her. But mostly she just wanted to keep her spirits up. "If I were going to die, I'd have done it already," she told herself. "I've got to get back to Papa."

She stopped for a moment, and slowly sucked a couple of the candies she had saved. The sharp tang of peppermint was comforting. She remembered, then, that this was Christmas Day. "Not much of a dinner," she thought, "and no presents." But she was still alive and maybe that was enough.

Then, as darkness fell over the jungle, Juliane thought of new terrors. Night in the jungle is full of strange sounds and rustlings in the bush. Juliane knew that animals gathered by the stream at night to drink. She didn't want to be around when the big cats arrived. It was time to think about finding a place to spend the night.

Moving a little way from the water, Juliane found a clearing. The leaves and branches of great trees kept the ground from being too soggy. Juliane first went over the area with her stick.

There were no snakes. Then she carefully raked what leaves she could into a bed.

She lay down, but sleep would not come. Every crackling in the bushes made her sit up in terror. Something large and fuzzy scurried over her legs. She let out a strangled scream. Was it a tarantula, a large hairy spider? The air was heavy. It smelled of rotting damp plants.

Juliane heard nightbirds calling to each other. She remembered how her mother could tell each bird by its call. Would she ever see her again? As

the night music echoed in her ears, Juliane sank into sleep. But many times during the night, some movement or sharp snap of a twig brought her wide awake. But she could see nothing, and she fell asleep again. She knew that without rest she would never be able to walk out of the jungle. And getting out alive seemed to be the only thing that mattered anymore.

CHAPTER 4

Walk Through Danger

Juliane awoke the morning of the third day still tired. For a moment she didn't know where she was. But then she remembered. She picked up her stick and arose. Slowly she made her way back to the stream. Juliane splashed her face with water. She tried to wash away some of the dirt that stuck to the open cut on her foot. The cold water seemed to make the insect bites on her arms and face itch more. She tried not to dig at them with her nails. Juliane set out again.

As she walked along, her ears picked up a new bird sound. It was the hoarse cry of vultures. Juliane knew what vultures meant, and she shivered. These birds live off dead bodies. Where there were vultures, there were usually bodies. Juliane followed the sounds and saw where the vultures were circling. They were near part of the airplane. Carefully she searched the area, frightened yet determined to discover if there was anyone, living or dead, that might have attracted the vultures. She called, peering into the bushes under which an injured person might have crawled for shelter. But she found nobody. She kept walking.

The stream became wider. Perhaps, Juliane thought, a large river was nearby now. And certainly, she also thought, someone must have started looking for the airplane by now. Suddenly her head jerked up, her eyes searched the sky. A noise was coming from above her—a plane!

Juliane quickly looked around. She tried to spot a clearing in which she could stand and wave her arms. But the tall trees of the jungle closed out the sky. There was no clearing.

Juliane listened. She could tell that the plane was circling. "It's a search plane," she thought, her heart thumping. "They're looking for me!"

She couldn't see the plane, and Juliane knew the searchers couldn't see her. But still she yelled out. "Hello!" she cried, over and over, stumbling wildly through the woods, trying to follow the sound. "Hello! Oh, please, let them hear me! Don't let them leave me alone!"

Gradually the sound of the plane faded away. Even so, Juliane kept shouting until she couldn't shout anymore. "They think we're all dead," she thought. "They think I'm dead." She didn't feel like moving.

But the will to live forced her to stand and go on. "I can still walk," she said out loud. "I'm not hungry, and I can drink from the stream. I'm not going to let this kill me!" She clenched her jaw to keep from crying as she began again to make her way along the stream.

On the fourth day, Juliane's Christmas candy ran out. She ate the last piece as slowly as she could, enjoying the sharp, sweet flavor. As she

did, she looked at her arms and legs. They were swelled with bites from horseflies and mosquitoes. "At least *they're* eating well," she thought.

Now a new danger faced her. Long streams of army ants now and then blocked her path. These ants are very dangerous. They eat meat, and they eat any animal that gets in their way. Juliane had to take long detours around the lines of army ants. This often took her far out of her way, wasting time and energy.

But Juliane was happy finally to see her little stream running into a large river. A river would mean villages and people. She moved on with new spirit.

Out of the corner of her eye, Juliane saw something move. She jumped back with a gasp. She jumped again as a huge toad landed with a plop in the mud near her feet. Then it leaped away. "Well at least toads don't bite," Juliane thought.

And she saw many of them as the day went on.

Juliane's legs felt weak. She knew her body needed food, although she didn't really feel hungry. Her mother had told her once that cooked frog's legs tasted good. If frog's legs could be eaten, what about toad's legs? Toads moved slowly, so they wouldn't be hard to catch. She saw a large one, sunning itself on a wet rock at the water's edge. Quietly, carefully, she crept up on it. Her hand darted out, but the toad moved faster and splashed into the water. She spotted another toad and tried again. This time she caught it. But as she held the wriggling toad in her hands, she began to feel sick. She threw it into the water. She would rather go hungry than eat *that*. And she had no way to cook it anyway.

Then Juliane spotted a tree full of fruit. She eagerly ran toward it. But then she stopped. She remembered that her parents had warned her against fruits and berries in the jungle she didn't know about. Many pretty plants held deadly poison. Juliane knew nothing about this fruit. She decided to pass it by, even though now her stomach rumbled with hunger.

CHAPTER
5

A Boat, A Hut, and Voices

Days passed. Juliane found no one. Flies laid eggs in the deep cut on her foot. The eggs hatched into wriggling white maggots that would grow into flies. The sight of them on her foot made Juliane sick. She feared they might eat her alive. She tried to pick them out. But she couldn't get them all, and she saw that her wound was growing larger now instead of healing. Her heart fell when she thought that even if she did survive, she might lose her foot. She tried to put that out of her mind. But every time she looked at her foot she felt weak and sick inside.

The river was getting wider and wider now. It ran more swiftly too. The water was also deeper. Wading into it, when she had to, became dangerous. Sometimes the fast-moving water made her stagger and fall. It swept her along a few yards before she could get back on her feet and on land again. The days were very hot.

Juliane was always wet, even out of the water. Maybe, she thought, it would be worth the risk to try to swim a little. The river would carry her along. She would not have to swim hard. The flies and mosquitoes would leave her alone. True, piranhas might get her, but she knew she wouldn't last much longer walking. She was becoming very weak.

Carefully she checked the river as far ahead as she could see. Then she waded out and began weakly to swim. It didn't call for much work, and Juliane thought mainly about keeping her head above water. It was almost fun. She relaxed and let the cool of the water seep through her body.

But she couldn't stay in long. For one thing, bends in the river made it impossible to see what lay ahead. And around any bend, a hungry caiman—an alligator—could be waiting. At last, grabbing a rock, she pulled herself to her feet and stepped onto the bank.

Hunger gnawed at her. Juliane tried to re-

member when she had last eaten, but it was hard to separate the days in her mind. They all seemed to run together. After some thought, she figured that this was her tenth day since the crash. Only ten days? It felt like ten years. Sometimes she wondered if there was anyone besides herself left alive in the world. Had she been spared only to walk until she dropped?

Another long day ended. Juliane searched for a clear spot in which to hide for another night. As she walked along a bend in the river, her eyes hit on something that made her blink, then cry out in happiness. A boat! A canoe, tied to a stump by the river. A boat meant people nearby. Near the boat, Juliane could make out a path, a path worn by human feet. Overcome with excitement, Juliane eagerly ran to it. Then she made another discovery. There, nestled in the trees, was a little hut. Juliane called out, but nobody answered or looked out. Slowly, she walked to the hut and stood in the doorway. She looked in.

All she saw was a little motor for a boat and a can of gasoline. Both looked as though they had been left there not long ago. Perhaps the hut's owners had gone out just for the day to hunt or fish. They might be back soon. Thankful for a roof over her head, Juliane sat down on the hard-packed dirt floor. Clouds were forming in the sky. Thunder rumbled. Rain would come soon.

With a sliver of wood, Juliane carefully dug out more maggots from her foot. It was so nice to look up and see something besides trees and vines. It was good to be indoors.

She lay down on the floor and tried to rest. But her sleep was troubled. Every time a bird screeched, every time an animal called, her eyes flew open. She hoped to see another human being. But each time there was no one there.

Perhaps, she thought, this hut was just another dead end. As night fell, she finally forgot her worries in sleep.

The next morning, Juliane awoke and stretched. Her body ached. Nobody had ap-

peared during the night. She had to live with the thought that it might be weeks before the owners of the hut came. They hadn't returned there to sleep, so they probably weren't nearby. She wondered if she should set out in the boat. But that might leave someone else no way to get out of the jungle. She didn't want to do that.

The rain poured down outside. The ground turned into slippery mud. Juliane knew she had to push on. To wait for help to come to her might mean dying of starvation in the hut. If there were people nearby, she had to get to them, somehow.

But it was awfully wet outside. The little hut was dry and cozy. Juliane sat back down on the floor. Perhaps, later in the day, the rain would let up. It couldn't hurt to wait a little longer. Bending over her foot, she tried to root out more maggots.

As she worked, Juliane's head jerked up in surprise. There were voices outside! Three men suddenly appeared in the hut. They looked in surprise at their unexpected guest. "What have we here?" one exclaimed.

CHAPTER 6

The Bad Dream Fades

As the three men stared at Juliane, she told them who she was and how she had come there. They could hardly believe that she was alive. All three had heard of the plane accident. One of them told her that he had flown in a search plane over the jungle, looking for survivors or pieces of the plane. But he had found nothing. Juliane remembered hearing the plane.

The three men were hunters who came into the jungle often. They traveled to and from their village on the river. The hut was one of several they kept to store goods. Juliane was lucky. They visited this hut only once every three weeks or so. It was just chance that they had found her when they did. There were no villages she could have reached from there on foot.

The men looked at Juliane's wounds. One of them opened the gasoline can and poured some over the maggots. This killed them, and Juliane dug out the rest of them. The men mixed salt in water and gently washed her body, now covered with sores and insect bites. The salt stung, but one man explained that it would help close the wounds and heal them. One of them dug into his knapsack and found a tube of salve, which eased the itching.

The men asked when she had last eaten. They couldn't believe that she had had nothing but candy, and only a little of that. One of them wanted to cook some meat for her right away. But another said, "Her belly is too weak. It would never hold it." One man went out into the

jungle, returning with an armload of ripe fruit. He urged Juliane to eat. But her stomach couldn't hold down even this. The men decided that they would start out the next morning for the nearest village downriver, Tournavista. That night Juliane had her first good sleep for a long time.

The next morning the four awakened at dawn. They climbed into the light canoe. Juliane laid back weakly as the three men paddled.

The river, named the Shebonya, was swift and wide. It seemed filled with rocks, over which the water tumbled. The canoe shook and quivered in the fast water. Juliane held tightly to the sides, terrified. It seemed impossible that the little boat would not go under or break into pieces on rocks. But the three men knew what they were doing. They had made this trip many times before.

The river joined another river, the Pachitea. Now the going was even swifter and more dangerous. And the sun had nearly set when they reached Tournavista. As the boat neared the riverbank, people came out of their huts to stare at the little boat's strange cargo. They ran, calling to their neighbors and pointing at Juliane. She couldn't understand what was going on until one of the hunters gently explained. Her eyes were so bloodshot that the whites had disappeared. Her

eyes were totally red. Her face was lumpy and swollen with insect bites. Worms had pitted her arms and legs with hideous sores. She looked like a monster.

Juliane was too weak to care about what anyone thought. She could hardly believe all that had happened. Had it been a dream? "If I woke up in the jungle again, I don't think I could stand it," she thought.

But it was no dream. The little boat bumped against the riverbank. One of the men jumped out and tied it to a post. Kind hands lifted Juliane out of the boat. A boy ran to tell the local doctor.

At the doctor's office, he and his nurse gave Juliane first aid.

"It was a good thing they found you when they did," the nurse said.

"We can only do the simplest kind of work on you here," the doctor explained. "You've got to have more treatment at a hospital."

"Please tell my father," Juliane begged weakly. The doctor promised he would.

Eleven and a half days after the accident, Juliane boarded a plane that flew her to Pucallpa. Her father was waiting there, and a doctor treated her. Juliane felt faint with relief when he told her that her foot would be all right. She would not lose it.

Juliane told her story to airplane pilots who

would search again for wreckage. Her directions helped them find it. Later, her father told her what she had suspected all along. Her mother was dead.

Searchers found that several of the passengers of Flight 508 had landed on the ground alive, too. But they had died quickly in the unfamilar jungle. Only Juliane, one out of ninety-two, had lived.

Afterward, it all seemed to Juliane like a bad dream that faded slowly from her memory. But the three hunters and the people of the little jungle village still remember the first shocking sight of Juliane's face. And they often tell the story of the one who was left alive.